The Wit and Wisdom of
West Highland Terriers

This is a STAR FIRE book created for LOMOND

STAR FIRE BOOKS
Crabtree Hall, Crabtree Lane
Fulham, London SW6 6TY
United Kingdom

www.star-fire.co.uk

First published 2007

07 09 11 10 08

1 3 5 7 9 10 8 6 4 2

Star Fire is part of The Foundry Creative Media Company Limited

The CIP record for this book is available from the British Library.

ISBN: 978 1 84204 129 1

Printed in China

Thanks to: Cat Emslie, Andy Frostick, Sara Robson,
Gemma Walters and Nick Wells

The Wit and Wisdom of
West Highland
Terriers

Ulysses Brave

LOMOND

Foreword

For years I studied Zen and the Art of
Animal Self-consciousness. Subsequently I
have written a large number of management,
self-help and philosophical texts over the
years, which have provided helpful advice
to those less fortunate than myself.
Here then, is my latest offering.

Ulysses Brave

Try to keep your head up if you're feeling low. Apart from keeping the hair from your eyes, it will instill confidence.

Confidence is the key to success. When hunting for friends or jobs, always walk with a ready smile and a straight back.

Try to avoid situations
which you find depressing.

Make some time every day to celebrate.

Fear is your greatest enemy. You can defeat it by remembering those who love you.

If you have trouble concentrating, just take five deep breaths and remain still for two minutes.

Be ready for action at all times, especially in the defence of your places of rest.

Sometimes the perfect colour
is simply not available.
Try not to put yourself
under too much pressure.

*Don't feel ashamed about
the silly things you do in the
privacy of your own home.*

Twins can be fun.

Curiosity can be a good thing.
Judgement is always better.

*If life seems to become
entangled, try to do something
completely different.*

There are times when we all want to sink into the background. Camouflage, correctly administered, can be useful.

Here we go again...

*Opening your lungs first
thing in the morning will
fill your body with
life-enhancing energy.*

The ancient art of moon-staring
can bring significant benefits
to the inner soul.

*Luxuries and privileges
can sometimes hold you back.
It is often better to fight for
what you want.*

Just focus on your goals...

...dont wait for events, leap towards them and wrestle them to the ground.

Going to a party can relieve the tension, even if it's the last thing you want to do.

Some people like parties!

Try to maintain a healthy diet.

If you bring a friend to
an important event,
make sure they don't
cramp your style.

*Watch and compose yourself
before you leap in. Success lies
in planning and poise.*

Dreaming of a better place can help you through the day.

Sometimes it's a great relief
to get to the end of the day.

*Keep your spine in a neutral
position for as long as you
can manage.*

*Try to leave the city
behind for a few hours
a week.*

*Some people will be
wary if you show too
much enthusiasm.*

Try to find a new challenge in your life.

*If you find yourself in
a tight corner, genuine
curiosity can be the most
disarming weapon.*

*All forms of Martial Arts
provide great discipline.*

You know a true friend
by their attitude to
your appearance.

See you soon...